# boat

**Boot**

# medicine

**Medizin**

# night

**Nacht-**

# snow

**Schnee**

sun

Sonne

cat

Katze

hair

Haar

flag

Flagge

## man

## Mann

## happy

## glücklich

## goodbye

## Auf Wiedersehen

## snake

## Schlange

paper

Papier-

pear

Birne

teach

lehren

alligator

Alligator

# dog

Hund

# pillow

Kissen

# eight

acht

# goat

Ziege

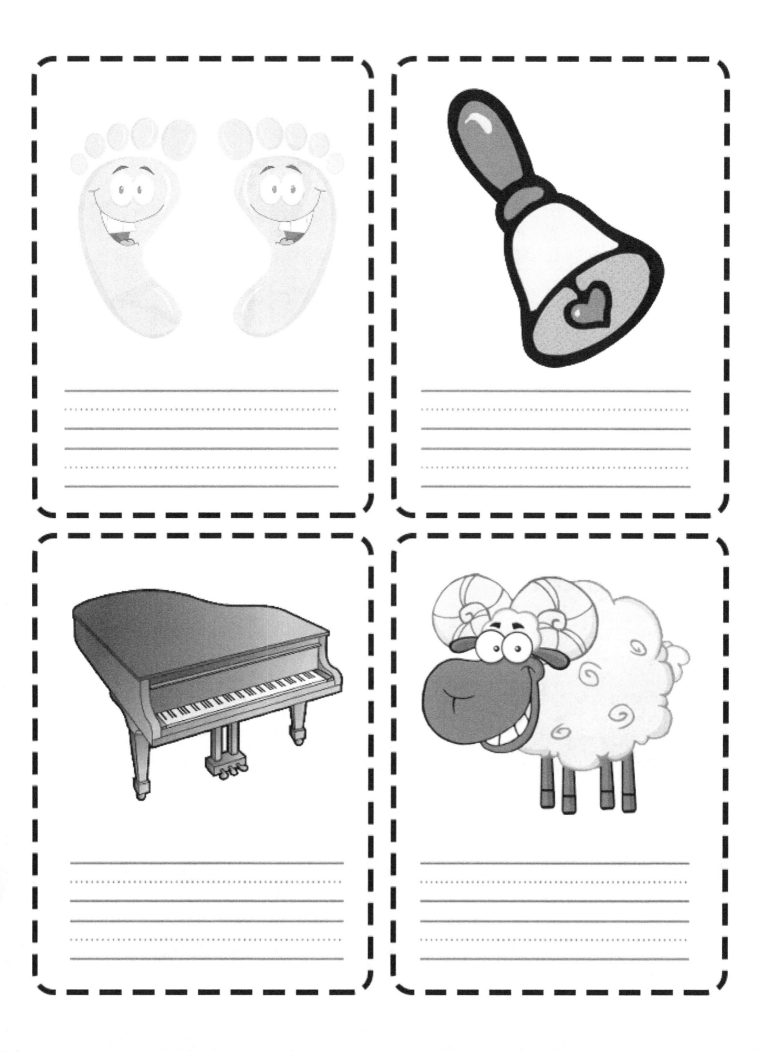

## foot

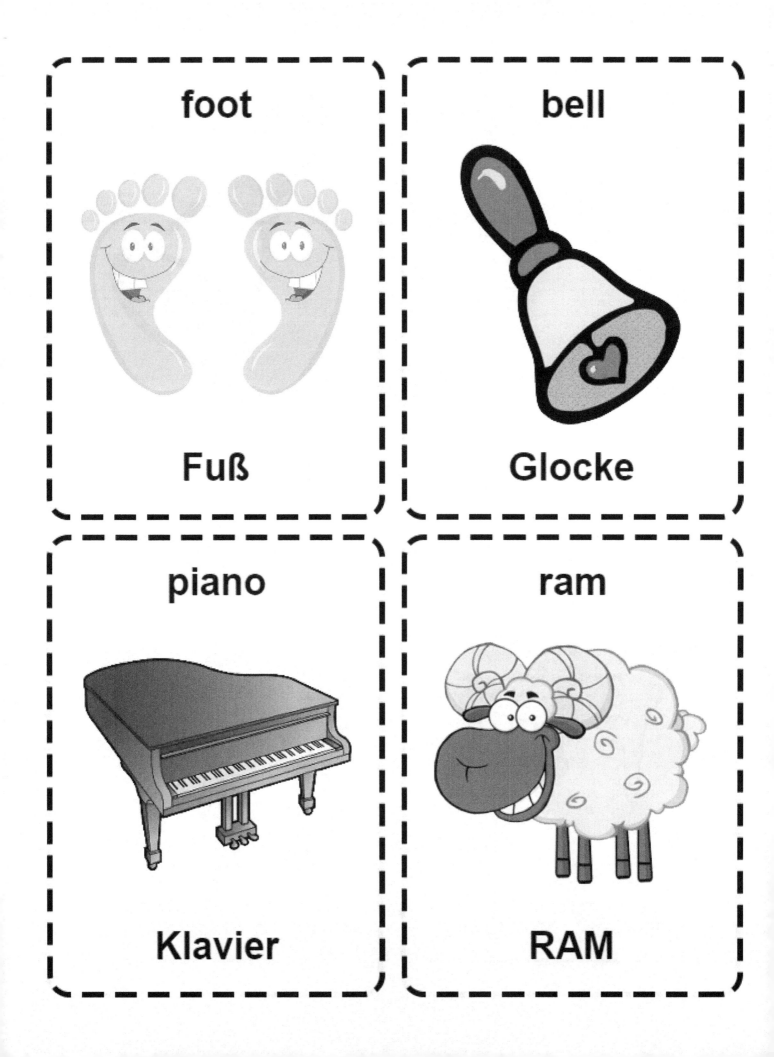

Fuß

## bell

Glocke

## piano

Klavier

## ram

RAM

## laugh

## Lachen

## mother

## Mutter

## question

## Frage

## truck

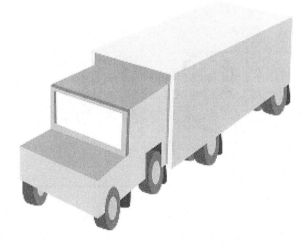

## LKW

## doctor

## Arzt

## car

## Auto

## strawberry

## Erdbeere

## train

## Zug

jet

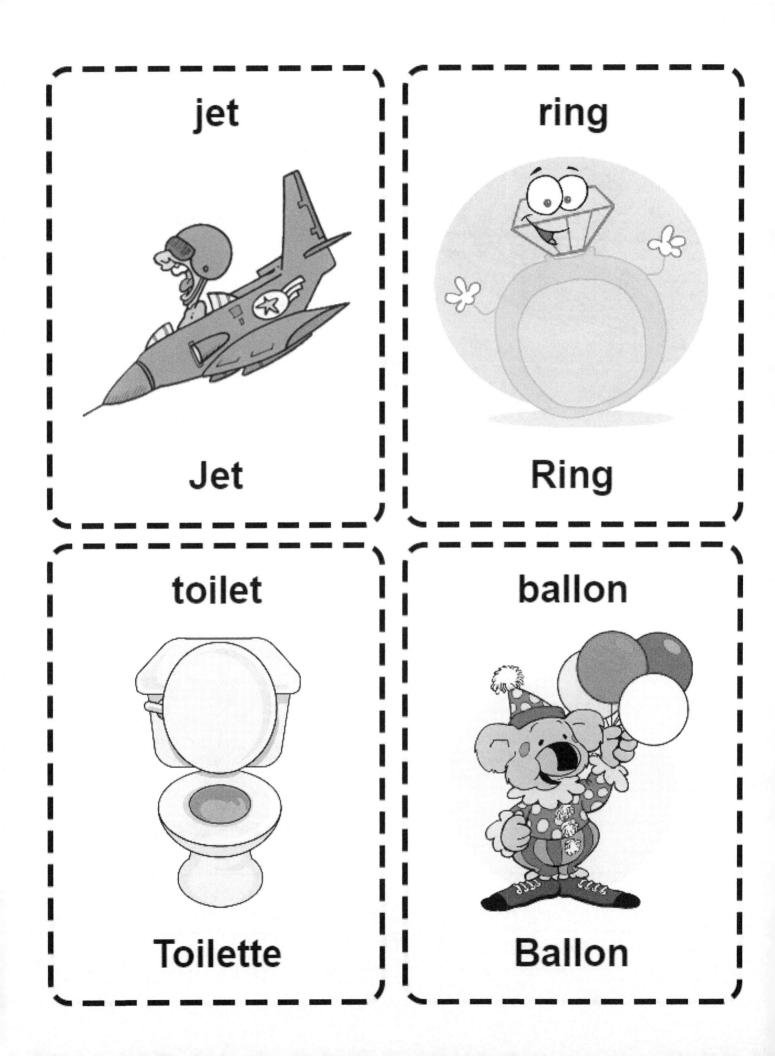

Jet

ring

Ring

toilet

Toilette

ballon

Ballon

# wake up

## aufwachen

# turkey

## Truthahn

# violin

## Geige

# yarn

## Garn

# love

## Liebe

# bag

## Tasche

# lemon

## Zitrone

# deer

## Hirsch

# hurt

**verletzt**

# earth

**Erde**

# bus

**Bus**

# hedgehog

**Igel**

# fish

Fisch

# zoo

Zoo

# worm

Wurm

# working

Arbeiten

# birthday

## Geburtstag

# clean

## sauber

# groundhog

## Murmeltier

# riding

## Reiten

# van

van

# bird

Vogel

# vase

Vase

# math

Mathematik

........................................................

........................................................

........................................................

........................................................

........................................................

........................................................

........................................................

........................................................

........................................................

........................................................

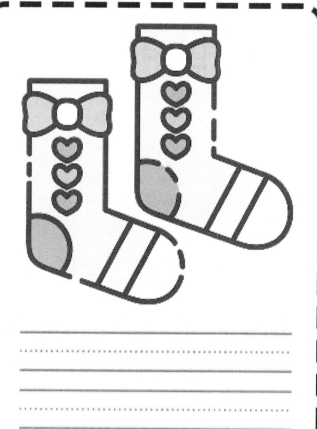

........................................................

........................................................

........................................................

........................................................

........................................................

........................................................

........................................................

........................................................

........................................................

........................................................

## bedroom

## Schlafzimmer

## read

## lesen

## socks

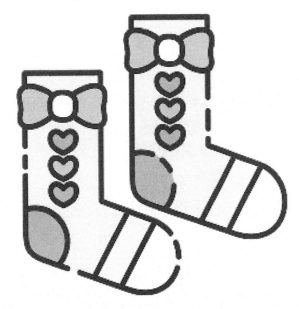

## Socken

## giraffe

## Giraffe

# owl

## Eule

# homework

## Hausaufgaben

# cherry

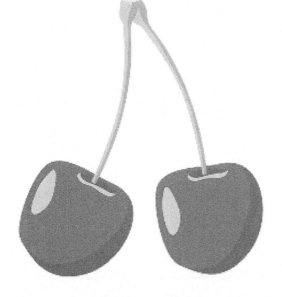

## Kirsche

# drum

## Trommel

| hand | baseball |
|:---:|:---:|
|  | |
| Hand | Baseball |
| seven | queen |
| Sieben | Königin |

## sleeping

## Schlafen

## bee

## Biene

## doll

## Puppe

## window

## Fenster

## water

Wasser

## win

Sieg

## cow

Kuh

## gun

Gewehr

jug

Krug

egg

Ei

hug

Umarmung

bone

Knochen

## three

**3**

drei

## plane

Ebene

## bird's nest

Vogelnest

## ant

Ameise

duck

Ente

moon

Mond

six

sechs

swimming

Schwimmen

## drawing

**Zeichnung**

## play

**abspielen**

## toothbrush

**Zahnbürste**

## home

**Zuhause**

baby

Baby

morning

Morgen

girl

Mädchen

presents

die Geschenke

shoe

Schuh

drink

Getränk

pan

schwenken

door

Tür

## coat

**Mantel**

## whale

**Wal**

## octopus

**Tintenfisch**

## ladybug

**Marienkäfer**

## durian

Durian

## zebra

Zebra

## two

zwei

## king

König

# lion

Löwe

# snail

Schnecke

# rooster

Hahn

# horse

Pferd

## squirrel

## Eichhörnchen

## elephant

## Elefant

## leg

## Bein

## icecream

## Eis

........................................
........................................
........................................
........................................

........................................
........................................
........................................
........................................

........................................
........................................
........................................
........................................

........................................
........................................
........................................
........................................

# wash

## waschen

# fire

## Feuer

# school

## Schule

# climbing

## klettern

# chicken

## Hähnchen

# cry

## Weinen

# sick

## krank

# tiger

## Tiger

## kangaroo

## Känguru

## sleepy

## schläfrig

## nine

## neun

## bicycle

## Fahrrad

## shark

## Hai

## yogurt

## Joghurt

## fall

## fallen

## sad

## traurig

## eat

**Essen**

## hen

**Henne**

## eye

**Auge**

## volcano

**Vulkan**

# toy

Spielzeug

# toothpaste

Zahnpasta

# banana

Banane

# rain

Regen

# singing

## Singen

# monkey

## Affe

# milk

## Milch

# jump

## springen

coconut

Kokosnuss

frog

Frosch

tree

Baum

bed

Bett

# comb

Kamm

# soccer

Fußball

# pig

Schwein

# orange

Orange

# playground

## Spielplatz

# run

## Lauf

# box

## Box

# book

## Buch

# xylophone

## Xylophon

# zero

## Null

# walk

## gehen

# farmer

## Farmer

_____
....................................................
_____
_____
....................................................
_____

_____
....................................................
_____
_____
....................................................

_____
....................................................
_____
_____
....................................................
_____

_____
....................................................
_____
_____
....................................................
_____

## unicorn

**Einhorn**

## shopping

**Einkaufen**

## suitcase

**Koffer**

## five

**fünf**

# bread

Brot

# one

ein

# cooking

Kochen

# four

vier

# money

Geld

# zipper

Reißverschluss

# sheep

Schaf

# umbrella

Regenschirm

## pineapple

Ananas

## yak

Yak

## flower

Blume

## jam

Marmelade

# breakfast

## Frühstück

# chair

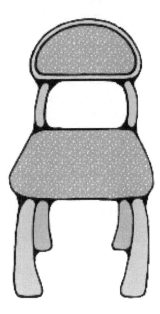

## Stuhl

# ball

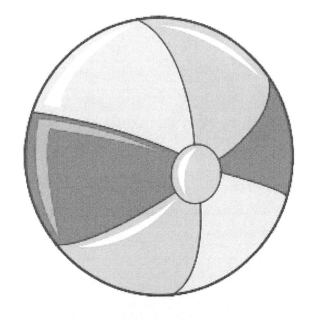

## Ball

# dressing

## Dressing

# children

Kinder

# corn

Mais

# ten

zehn

# gift

Geschenk

## writing

## Schreiben

## apple

## Apfel

## friend

## Freund

## ironing

## Bügeln

## rabbit

## Hase

## wind

## Wind

## father

## Vater

## watermelon

## Wassermelone

## sister

## Schwester

## shower

## Dusche

## cake

## Kuchen

## brother

## Bruder

Made in the USA
Columbia, SC
27 May 2019